The Ups and Downs of Love
Love is Like the Lines
on an EKG

@ardreanathompson

The Ups and Downs of Love: Love is Like the Lines on an EKG
Poems by: Ardreana Thompson

Cover by: Jazzy Kitty Publishing
Designed by: Jazzy Kitty Publishing
Logo Designs by: Andre M. Saunders/Leroy Grayson
Editor: Anelda L. Attaway

© 2016 Ardreana Thompson
ISBN 978-0-9970848-1-8
Library of Congress Control Number: 2016934519

All rights reserved. This book is protected under the copyright laws of the United States of America. No part of this publication may be reproduced or transmitted in any format or by any means electronic, mechanical, or otherwise, including photocopying, recording or any other storage or retrieval system without written permission of the publisher, except in the case of brief quotations embodied in critical articles or reviews.

For Worldwide Distribution. Printed in the United States of America. Published by Jazzy Kitty Greetings Marketing & Publishing, LLC. Utilizing Microsoft and Adobe Publishing Software. Utilizing Adobe and Microsoft Publishing Software.

ACKNOWLEDGMENTS

To be thankful and grateful for anything that life has thrown my way, I had to understand that love has its ups and downs. Through it all, I've remained genuine and true to my emotions under every single circumstance. These are the things that never fail to make me who I am.

I'll never stop thanking God for everything that He's done and everything that He's going to do for me.

I would like to thank the women who at some point in time in my life served as mother figures although they were of no blood relation nor under any obligation to do so. My appreciation is extended to the late Mrs. Jacqueline Allison-Savage, Ms. Lillie Bell Higginbottom, Mrs. Brenda Sims, Mrs. Mary Eaton and last but certainly not least Mrs. Lisa Johnson.

I'm thankful and forever grateful for meeting Lionel Saulsberry and Janice Robbins at the Dallas County Health Department in Selma, AL. They have supported me every step of my career and no words nor any dollar amount would be enough to thank them for all that they've done for me.

Ms. Faye Sheffield has been one of the most remarkable people I've ever met. During my crying days, she was there to help dry every tear. When she looks at me today, I know that I look like a brand new person. Indeed, I am!

I would like to thank one of my newest sisters Kiera Clark. We've only known each other for a short amount of time, but it feels as if we've known each other for an eternity. We met on the set of the movie "Selma" which was filmed in Selma, AL where we worked as background artist. Then and there, we knew that we were different from the rest of the world because for us to be so young, we saw the visual concept of the civil rights movement in the exact same way. We are truly long lost sisters.

I would like to thank the Wilcox County and Dallas County/Selma Chapter of National Council for Negro Women for helping to mold me into a productive young woman.

I would like to thank my childhood best friend, Veronica Eaton for still being in my life, even after twenty plus years. That type of loyalty is difficult to find in this day and time, but by the grace of God, we pulled it off.

I could never stop thanking my current best friend Tiffany Hartley. She's more than just my friend, she's also a sister to me.

I am thankful for all of the relationships that have taught me to be a woman. I am truly grateful and touched by every woman, man, boy, and girl who has become a fan of mines by reading, listening, or just simply watching what I do.

Finally, I would like everyone in my life to know that if you are still here throughout all of the ups and downs, you are considered my family. It is you who have made a difference in my life and no drop of blood could tell me anything different. Thank you!

DEDICATIONS

This Book is Dedicated to the Love of my Life...

My nephew whom I've watched grow from a new born to a big energetic, amazing 11-year-old...

Darryl "Boo" Tolbert Jr. (My Big Baby!)

TABLE OF CONTENTS

Introduction	i
Phase I – Love is a Terrible Thing to Waste	01
Love is a Terrible Thing to Waste	02
A Time to Be Pressured	06
Do You Remember?	11
Nothing at All	16
Doll-Like Life	20
Will I End Up Lonely?	22
Intact Emotions	27
Too Late	31
Tragic	37
Unconvinced	42
He Fell Asleep	46
Another Level	49
You Created Me	51
I'll Never Love Again	53
Damaged Goods	56
Never Learned How to Love	59
A Woman's Growth	64
Finding Love	68
Resigned Loved	71
The Only One Playing	73
A Good Woman's Blues	75

TABLE OF CONTENTS

Phase II – The Mistakes of Love	78
The People We Used to Be	81
Burned Bridges	85
My Trail of Tears	88
The Quit Before the Loss	90
Closed Walls	95
In Love with Someone Else	98
Pages Within My Notebook	101
Wanting a New Heart	104
Unforgiven	107
Phase III – Never Stop Loving	109
Never Say Never	110
"A Natural Thing	113
Your Love	115
My Heart	118
Some Day	122
Love Is	124
Unconditional	126
A Second Chance	129
The Song of Our Love	132
Overthrown Queen	135
Something About Your Love is Beautiful	137
Glass of Wine	141

TABLE OF CONTENTS

Accepting Him 142

Love Made a Liar Out of Me 145

Again 147

Forever... 152

My Blessing... 157

A Never Ending Love... 159

Your Presence.. 163

Topic of Discussion.. 164

Undefiled Sheets... 168

Wish Upon a Star 171

About the Author.. 173

INTRODUCTION

After many attempts of expressing my views on the things that I thought I wanted to write about, I finally built the nerves to begin penning the words to what I needed to write about. Many nights, I lie down heavy hearted as I search for the understanding that I need. It seems that it's the only way for me to find closure about many emotional issues pertaining to love.

Sometimes I wonder about the actions of others, which leads me to question the actions of my own self. Could a person be reacting off of my actions or is my reaction to the action of another the correct action?

I'm no philosopher, but I love the philosophies of life. Ultimately, I love the mysteries that begin to unravel as we live. Too many of us are not paying attention, but my hat goes off to the soul who thinks it's worthwhile to do so. For some, I can honestly vouch and say that they want to pay attention, but truly don't know how to.

The phrase, "Knowledge is power", has deemed itself true. We live recklessly when we don't know any better. There's a proverb that says, "People perish from the lack of knowledge," and there's no better way to say it. Therefore, I've finally succumbed to the impression that when we self-educate ourselves on the subject of self and the subject of love, we can advance.

Everyone seems to think that they know what love is, but I can honestly say that too many people are ignorant about the topic. I'm not claiming to know everything about it myself, but I know enough to know what it's not. If everyone understood what love was, there wouldn't be so many divorces. To marry someone, any sane person would at least have to think that they have at least an ounce of love for the person that they've chosen to marry. We must all come to understand that we marry because we love and not find love because we get married. We must also understand that love is not simply a feeling, but an overall outline to our actions.

On a more spiritual level, love is explained. It may be difficult to carry out, but it's explained. Love is long suffering. It hangs in there with you through the good and the bad. Love is kind. It will treat you right. Love does not envy. It will not boil over with anger to get something that you have. Love does not puff itself up. It will not make itself out to be more just to make you feel small. Love does not behave unseemly. It will not act out of the characteristics of what it truly is. Love is not selfish. It is not self-seeking and will have more than its own interest at heart. Love is not easily provoked. It will be patient when under pressure. Love thinketh no evil. It will not wish evil upon you.

Love rejoiceth in the truth. Its joy comes from pure honesty. Love beareth all things. It's there through thick and thin. Love believeth all things, endureth all things, and last but not least, love never fails.

A large number of people don't understand love; therefore, when someone comes along and loves them the right way, it's foreign to them. Ignorance causes them to act foolishly. Sometimes, people walk all over those who truly loves them. There have been times that I've heard people complain about what someone did to them in the past and then turn right around and do the same to another person. Over time, I've learned that a person who doesn't truly understand love will be more likely to reject the person who loves them. Out of fear, they are likely to be rude. Although it's tough to endure the hate that has to exit one's heart in order for love to enter in, it's worth it because the giver must understand that the receiver doesn't understand what's happening. There is a very true saying that says, "People often fear what they don't understand." Therefore, love is one of the most feared occupants of this earth.

As time progresses, my heart grows more and more weary when dealing with love. It seems as though the more people we give our love to, the less love that we possess for ourselves. As humans, we tend to believe that we must stop the flow of love in order to live a productive life. In a sense, it's understandable because I can't count the number of times that I've just wanted to give up in finding it. I can't lie, sometimes I still wonder if it's just better for me to be alone for the rest of my life, but for a lack of better words, that's kind of silly. In a retrospect, I know that I always will need love in order to live productively. We're all so hung up on some type of fairy tale and pixie dust dream which is nothing more than sugar coated lust that has been dressed up and served as love.

Very often, we are blinded by our own selfish wants. We constantly think that if one makes us feel good, then they must love us. That is untrue because the purest acts of love have derived from instances that didn't feel so good to the receiver. I'm not so sure that in any case of discipline whether the person being disciplined or the disciplinarian are at his or her happiest mood, but I'm almost sure that the disciplinarian understands the future of the person being disciplined is more important than just a pleasant moment.

If you love someone, you tell them the truth no matter how much it hurts them. If they can't understand the truth, you show them no matter how much it hurts you. There's no doubt in my mind that the lesson of the prodigal son was a hard one;

nevertheless, it was the best way for the father to teach it. Letting someone learn on their own is one of the best ways to teach those who you love that the grass is not always greener on the other side.

A person normally knows before the teacher that the lesson has properly been taught and a teacher normally knows before the student how effective the lesson will be on that individual. Although love has many different aspects, it's simple to understand. However, the methods of developing it can sometimes be difficult. Overall, I'm convinced that if you sit down and analyze love in its entirety, it will only be as difficult as you make it.

I believe that we often times struggle with love because we have become so insistent upon forcing it. I've learned over time that love can't be forced. If someone forces love, they need to understand that it's not real. Why would anyone want something as precious as love to be a knock off or counterfeit anyway?

As we get older, we learn more. When you know better, you do better. Some of us know better and still won't do any better. The term for that is stupidity. Nevertheless, in our youth, we all have been stupid. However, with life comes experiences and through those experiences we overcome mistakes. Our mistakes guide us into maturity which is nothing more than purchased wisdom. Wisdom is often emphasized by the things in life which we will never forget. Therefore, I think it's safe to say that the most unforgettable things in life are those things that have caused us the most pain.

Pain has made some of the best of us bitter. Many of us have become fearful, but a wise man knows how to take the dirt that has accumulated in life and grow a flower. Pain is one of the best things that has ever happened to me. For without misery, how would I know happiness, and without a wilderness to wander through, how could I have grown faith, patience, and endurance. The allowance of these things mold us into the finest of diamonds.

It's true that most people don't normally miss a good thing until it's gone. There's a quote that says, "Distance makes the heart grow fonder", but to what extent is that to be held true? There have been plenty of people whom I've distanced myself from and I'm not a bit fonder of them now than I was of them then. The truth is, sometimes we grow selfish when we become comfortable with a person. We think that they'll be here forever regardless of how bad we treat them or how horrible we make them feel. When they decide that enough is enough, pick up the pieces, and search for a better life, that's the only time that we realize how much their presence meant to us. That very moment could very well be a moment too late.

I believe that love is often frowned upon because of those who take advantage of it. We often complain about how much we hate love, but is love really what we hate? Love is not the one who's hurting us, people are. There are certain characteristics harbored by some of the people whom we fall in love with that hurts us. Greed, selfishness, anger, and harshness are only a few. We must learn to confront others about their hurtful characteristics. If you love someone, then you help them to work on their flaws. If a person is unwilling to work towards a better relationship with you, there is clearly a level of disrespect and you should move on. If a person matures over time and decides to come back with a better mindset, as fair enough as it is, people have been proven to change. Nevertheless, you should never allow anyone to interrupt your life whenever they feel like it. Make them get back in line and wait their turn. If they never get another chance, it's fine because they should have thought it worthwhile to cherish their chance while they had it.

In conclusion, sometimes we expect too much out of love. We will never find the perfect person, but where there are two people with imperfections, there's an opportunity for perfection as a couple. There's a chance for perfect moments. A person with one leg is deemed handicapped, but a person with two legs has a greater chance at perfect mobility. Therefore, we must learn to walk together in love, faith, and hope. With that being said, all we can do is hope to become the best couple of imperfections that we could possibly be.

Love is Like the Line on an EKG

Love is like the line on an EKG. It always has its ups and downs. Although we sometimes fix our mouths to say what we'll never do or what we won't do again, one can never really be sure of what the future holds. Overall, I believe that love is an experiment. At some point and time in life, we all will fall into the trap of becoming love's guinea pig, but as the old saying goes, "It's better to have loved and lost, than to never have loved at all." So I encourage you to experience love with full force and get back up when it knocks you down.

PHASE I

Love is a Terrible Thing to Waste

I wasted so much of my time and love on guys who did not have my best interest in mind. If young women would only listen to half of the things that I am telling them about love, then they would avoid a lot of pain.

LOVE IS A TERRIBLE THING TO WASTE

LOVE IS A TERRIBLE THING TO WASTE

And Hate is a terrible thing to Face

Sometimes I feel like I'm running a Rat Race

So I'm declaring that a Man...

Is a terrible thing to Chase

I don't ever want to find Myself

Chasing something So Replaceable

In my Book,

Being Desperate for a Man is...

Quite Distasteful

These guys can get with it

Or get lost in the System

If he treats me like a Dog

Why should I fix my Emotions to MISS him?

I don't Dismiss relationships for Simple Mistakes

But my Standards are High

And I'm steady Raising the Stakes...

To elements That sit far Above the Stars

So far Above the Heavens

That it peeps over at Mars

Like the Cellular Division

I'm constantly raising Bars

Because I'm DEEP like

A Caesarian Section

Leaving my Scars

I LOVED him

When they HATED him

I GAVE to him

As they TOOK from him

They rushed him Out of the Door

So I sat there and WAITED for him

The entire relationship turned me Bipolar

100 degrees' outside

But I was steady getting Colder

He asked me to be Kind

And then he asked me to be Bolder

I was pacing the Earth

As if I had a CHIP on my Shoulder

When all I really wanted him to do was

JUST LOVE ME

Instead,

He made it so that his Presence

Could DISGUST me

So I Wasted my Time

On someone who

WASN'T WORTH IT

And I Wasted my Love on someone

Who didn't DESERVE IT!

A TIME TO BE PRESSURED

I wish that I could

Exchange Spirits with you

For only a Day

So that I can Convince myself

That You Love me

But in a Different Kind of Way

I wish that I could

Open up your Mind

So that you can Climb

Out of this Box

And pay attention to Time

My Time is Precious

And I know that you know that

Your time is Precious

And that is the Reason that

You can't stand being Pressured

I can't Stand for my Time to be

Taken for Granted

Because my Time can't be Measured

If you would Open your Eyes

And peer beyond the Texture

You could see that I want you for

More than JUST Pleasure

Some are in Love with

The feeling of being Loved

And the feeling of

NOT being Lonely

Those people have been Deceived

Because in an Essence

Those feelings are Phony

Women who said they wanted you

Were only in Lust

Understand that I NEED YOU,

And that you can Trust

Loving God FIRST

And me Next is a Plus

Trying to do this thing without Him

Is nothing more than a Curse

I long to be with you

For Better or for Worst

I'll love you on my Feet

Or Face up in a Hearse

That means that I'll love you past

The day that I Die

I'll love you through the Smile

As well as through the Cry

If I have to Weigh things out
Through Deception and Lies
Then I guess I'll be Deceived
Until the Sweet By and By

I know like you know that
Pressure you Dislike
But God pressured the Sun
Until the Day became Night

If Pressuring you will Transform
Your Wrongs into Rights
Then I'll apply So Much Pressure
That my Pressure will Affects your Life

I'm pressuring you to
Not Take Time for Granted
Creating a line through my Heart
That appears to be Slanted

I'm still Hoping and Praying that

Later isn't Too Late

Advising me to Wait

But when you Wait...

Hearts Break

And when this Heart is Broken

My Heart will Remain Open...

For the Next Best Thing

So if I'm Worth being your Woman

Then I'm Worth wearing your Ring

DO YOU REMEMBER?

DO YOU REMEMBER?

When you told me that

You would NEVER forget about me?

You didn't Lie

Because I know that your Conscience cringes

At the thought of your Loss EVERYDAY

Even a Blind man could see that

You're Lost WITHOUT ME

I brought more Sunshine to your Life than

The Month of May

DO YOU REMEMBER?

When you told me that

I was the Best Thing that ever happened to you?

You didn't Lie

Because I brought Definition to your Life

Even a Deaf man have heard of how

I spoke Life to you

I'm Blessed to have DODGED the Bullet

Of being your Wife

DO YOU REMEMBER?

When you told me that

I deserved to be Happy?

You didn't Lie

Because I've been through more CRAP

Than the toilet Alone

I had Dreams;

Dreams that you Destroyed

You wasted this Love

Until it was eventually Gone

DO YOU REMEMBER?

When you told me that I was a Strong Woman?

You didn't Lie

Because I lifted the Weight from your Shoulders

With my Bare Hands

You knew that I brought Love whenever

You saw me Coming

But you never thought that my Type

Would one day be in High Demand

DO YOU REMEMBER?

When you told me that you Prayed to be with me?

You didn't Lie

Because God answered your Prayers

One Too Many Times!

I climbed the Highest Mountain

To be with you

And still you couldn't complete

The Simple Task of Making me Happy

Was it not possible for you to

Read between the lines?

DO YOU REMEMBER?

How I longed for you to Love me?

Instead all you did was Desert me

DO YOU REMEMBER?

How I tried to make it Work?

All you did was Aspire to make me Hurt

DO YOU REMEMBER?

How I gave you ALL of my Love?

You were my Life Support

And yet you Pulled the Plug

I thought that you FELL IN LOVE with me

Maybe I was too Blind to see.

That you were only Pretending to be

The person who you thought I Wanted you to be

When in Reality you couldn't Pretend to be

Your own Clone

Because you would still be

THE BIGGEST FRAUD

That the World has ever known

NOTHING AT ALL

My Soul feels as if it's Melting away

Dead to the World as I watch it Decay

I said to you, "I LOVE YOU"

And what did you Say?

NOTHING AT ALL,

You had Nothing to Say

I sat by the River

And Watched the currents at Flow

I created this River as my Tears fell Below

After all of these Tears,

What did I have to Show?

NOTHING AT ALL,

I had Nothing to Show

I peaked at the Sun
Through the Blinds of my Window

Surrounded by Heartache
And striking Pain at the Center
I proceeded to let you Enter
And what did you Remember?

NOTHING AT ALL,
You had Nothing to Remember

I suddenly broke down
At the Blow of the Wind
The beginning of my Life
Had caught up with the End

There was NOTHING more to do,
What was there for me to do?

NOTHING AT ALL

I had Nothing to do

NOTHING AT ALL

You had Nothing to say

"I LOVE YOU"

Were the words that Slowly

Pushed you away

NOTHING AT ALL,

I had Nothing to Show

Nothing but a river of Tears

Gathered Below

NOTHING AT ALL,

You had Nothing to Remember

You Never remembered to Appreciate me

From January to December

NOTHING AT ALL,

I had Nothing to do

But get myself Together

And give NOTHING to you

DOLL-LIKE LIFE

Been used up until Nothing was Left
Played with like a Doll
And put back on the Shelf

Hair Napped from your Combs
A permanent Facial Expression left Alone

All other Dolls remained Boxed
But my value is Done
NO VICTORIES WON
I can never be Number One

My moon doesn't Glow
No energy from my Sun
But you Never cared, Did you?
You never said, "I MISS YOU"

No Love

Never a reason to Hug

Nor Kiss you

Because you Never found a Reason

To be CONCERNED about me

No books with my Knowledge

How could you Learn about me?

The only Candle left on the Shelf seems

TO BURN WITHOUT ME

While those Glasses on your Eyes

See all Except me

So I'm all out of use

This is FINALLY the Finale

And my Doll-Like Life is OVER

So you're Done with me, SADLY

WILL I END UP LONELY?

Solely, my Sole Blows Slowly in the Wind

Gone Home to be all Alone

Where the walls Close In

PRETENDING?

That's not me!

FAKE?

Why be?

Honest lies Lie in your Eyes

I'm wondering how you See

A strong Storm is your Silence

There born is Peaceful Violence

And all of your Fullness

Suddenly seems so Condense

At first I was Convinced

But now I can't be Sure

The Aroma of your Absence

Smell worse than Manure

You said that you'd be True to me

Promised me what was Due me

Provided me with an Aura

That was more than Something New to me

Intelligence

Ignorance

Head on Collision

Trust

Lust

Dead wrong Decision

Touching the Screen of your Soul
Like a Smart Phone

Downloading, Blue-toothing,
Networking, Facebooking,
Tweeting, deleting your Files
Crashed databases

Haven't been here in a while
Momentarily wowed
Because I can't Climb out

Suddenly getting the Urge to
Just up and Put you out of my Life
How can I be your Wife?

How can I bear the Baby Girl?
That you so Confidently asked me for?

When you ignore my Text at Night

And I think, Oh Damn, you're Asleep

Can't feel these Emotions right

And I'm like Oh Damn,

I'm Weak

Constantly talking to myself Oh Damn,

I'm a Freak

Silence born before your Ears

And I think Speak Mouth,

Speak!

But mouth won't Speak

Because Heart's not in it

And body won't Move

Unless Soul Moves with it

I admit, I'm not even in it
But I'm caught up in the Moment
So eager to want to Own it

And thinking Damn
Again, I'll only end up Lonely

INTACT EMOTIONS

Nothing about my EMOTIONS

Are INTACT

In fact,

The Emotions that causes me to Love

Are filled with

Cuts, Scrapes, and open Sores

They no longer Protect me from Diseases

That fill my Heart

Leaving my Heart to Constantly be Broken

By the Man whom I Love the Most

These Emotions can

No Longer fight off

Incurable diseases that attack my Heart

Like AIDS

This Heart used to Produce Emotions

That act as T-Cells

Allowing the Opposite Sex to know

That I will Not and Cannot

Put up with Hurt

At this moment my Heart

No longer Works

So Emotions play on my Mind instead

Placing me in a State of Depression

That I don't know if I can Heal from

I can No Longer shed Tears

I can only Internalize these Feelings

And become Callous

My Heart has turned to Stone

Not to say that I can't Love Anymore

I just can't Love Properly

My mind Loves

But not by the Standards of my Heart

The mind is capable of Insanity

The Heart is what kept me Sane

So I declare

That my Sanity disappeared

With every Spirit of Love

That was Stored in my Heart

None of my EMOTIONS

Remain INTACT

These Cuts, Scrapes,

And open Sores

Bleed until they Can't Anymore

This Heart can No Longer

Pour out Feelings

I'm Numb and Immune to

ALL Love Potions

Because I lost my first Barrier

INTACT EMOTIONS

TOO LATE

I'm leaving

And there's NOTHING MORE to say about it

I've been Trapped in this Relationship

Feeling like an Inmate

Seeing my Life pass

As I peer through the Metal Gates

Closed behind these Iron Bars

You're my Cellmate

I'm buried in mental Scars

Bruised from the Wars

But still we choose to Fight

I've lost Sight of who I was

As a Free Woman

I used to be so Innocent

Yes, I was Innocent

Yet Sentenced to a Life of Imprisonment

For something that I was NEVER Guilty of

You locked me here as a result of your Insecurities

Constantly accusing me of a World of Impurities

You Lowered my Self-esteem

To where you Wanted it to be

I was Blinded by your Falsehood

And Mistaken Identity

But I will Never AGAIN Believe the Lies

Looking back,

I couldn't see through the Tears

In my Eyes

I was Verbally abused

And Beaten by your Fist of Envy and Rage

Misused beneath the Spotlight

As I stood on your Stage

Pain was there for the World to See

There was Weakness Inside of me

I longed for much more than your

Anger Filled Words…

"You're a Nasty Dirty Slut!"

"I HATE YOU!"

"Losing some weight would be Clever!"

"You're Ugly!"

"You DISGUST me!"

"It's a shame that I can't even use you

For my Pleasure!"

"You'll never be able to Love me!"

"How could you when your Womb can't even
Hold a Baby!"

So as I sat on the floor Crying

My insides were slowly Dying

Face Swollen

Nose Broken

I finally screamed, "I'M DONE with you!"
You yelled back, "No one else will ever love you!"

I Believed It!
I was deceived into thinking that your Treatment
Was Good Medicine

My body Bled as ink bleeds from a Pen
I was still pretending that my Heart would Mend
At the sound of one Insincere Apology

You forced me to Believe

That this was newer than Technology

So I succumbed to every Broken Bone,

Every Bloody Garment, and every put down

That You became so Comfortable issuing out to me

Damn, I'm so Stupid that

I can't even go back to my Family

Buried alive inside of a Room

Feels like I live inside of a Cage

I'm waiting for these Wounds to Heal

No one has seen me in Days

This is the Breaking Point

I'm leaving before Tomorrow becomes

A Day TOO LATE!

As my Palm wraps around the Door Knob

Your Fist collides into my Face

I fall to the Floor

My body takes on another Shape

You Forcefully pull me Apart

You Administer another Rape

No one's here to Save me

I guess I Forgot to tell you that

I was Pregnant with your Baby

Blacked out, Unconscious,

Coma, Brain dead

I'm leaving

I left,

But Unfortunately I LEFT DEAD!

TRAGIC

I've learned to be

A Woman over time

Broken hearts and Battered dreams

Leave Healed minds

As I set before the Last Man

Who tried to SELL ME

His version of why it's Wise for me...

To Trust his Sales Pitch

Of how I'm going to Enjoy Leaving

My Secretions on his SHEETS

And his Deletion I won't be...

My mind Slowly paddled

back to the Ocean of Deceit

Where I LOST my Virginity

My NOW and THEN seemed similar
Similarities intertwined with Clarities

I could see the inner Surface
That Rotted the surface like Cavities
It was a TRAGEDY

It's funny how "Boys to Men"
Isn't just a Song or Group
But where does the Transition begin
Where men gain their Couth?

"It's your choice," is what he said
As I lay with him in Bed
Open Hearts were there to Dread
Closed mind and Open legs in my Head...

Is where he was
Counterfeit was his Love

But he held enough Mind to Place

His hand inside of a Glove

There I was a Young and Foolish girl

Naively believing in Love

And he just thought that it was Cool

For him to get a good Cut

Society quoted, "Oh that's what's up."

He pissed his life into a Cup

Because lies meant nothing more to him

But a come up on his Luck

Lucky him Right?

I'm stupid for Desiring the Truth

And Trusting in individuals

Who tell me that they're True

But you're Praised for being a Liar

Isn't that the most Rewarding thing about you?

You're able to Manipulate

The World into Believing

That you're better than Trash

It's TRAGIC how you're a MAN

For being No Good

But I'm less than a WOMAN

For being Good

Would rewrite the Rules if I could

But it's OK

I'd rather be Misunderstood than to be

Societies definition of Good

Because now I know Better

I Do Better

I write words with No Letters

Because this life gets NO BETTER

I'm a Woman

Even if No One else Admits it

You're NOT a Man

I just hope that the World...

Finally Gets It!

UNCONVINCED

Last Night was my Last Night

To Cry over you

Like a Fool, I allowed you to Rule the Castle

You spear headed the Battle

But instead of you Uplifting me

You'd rather be my Master

A Disaster is what we're Involved in

Hurricanes throughout this Land

You cut my Legs away from me

And now I Can't Even Stand

I can't Stand up for Myself

I can't Stand up for my Rights

I can't stand Toe to Toe with my Opponent

In this Fight

Handicapped by the Words," I love you"

Sick from it like the Flu

If you really Loved me,

You wouldn't Treat me the way that you do

You allowed me to Drive a Car

On slick Tires

You allowed me to Burn in a House

That was on Fire

But you told the World

That you tried to Save me

I know that you're a Liar

YES, I SAID IT

It was you who saw me Begging

And yet you wouldn't even Stop the car

So that I could put my Leg in
Spoken Symbolically
Too late for your Apology

You got me feeling Second Hand
Like I'm NOTHING MORE
Than a Commodity

You should be Ashamed
Why would you ask to Marry me?
You can't even show that you would
Attempt to Take care of me

I'm NOT Materialistic
I don't' want you for your Money
But Honey
At least make me Believe that
You would TRY to be there for me

What if somehow I Needed you to be my Hero?

Question: Would you Marry me?

Answer: Hell No!

Maybe the Next woman will get Better than me

Because I'm certainly NOT Convinced

That you'd Take care of my Needs

HE FELL ASLEEP

We're Playing Games with each other

Neither one of us wants to Own the title

"LOVER"

We love in Dark colors

He stated, "I want you so bad."

I replied, "Same here."

I blew it off as the Wind

That demanded the Smoke to clear

He asked if he could Meet me

Eyes wide wanting to See me

Somewhere in the Crevices of my Mind

I was Convinced that other women Wanted to be me

He spoke nothings to me Sweetly

He did his thing Discretely

I must be Honest with myself,

I was feeling him Secretly

So he decided to Invite me on a Date

He made me Wait, Wait, and Wait

I checked my Phone for Text messages

And tried to determine our Fate

Hate formed in my Thoughts

Regret formed on my Face

I text him with the Urge

But the Circumstances of Us was

Really Not Up for Debate

The text read,

"YOU SHOULD SAY WHAT U MEAN

AND MEAN WHAT U SAY...
NEVER AGAIN TELL ME THAT YOU'RE GOING 2 DO
SOMETHING WHEN YOU KNOW THAT IT ISN'T TRUE

DAMN, IT'S ME ISN'T IT?
BE A MAN AND TELL THE TRUTH
I LOCKED UP MY HEART
AND THREW THE KEY AWAY"

Twenty minutes later he sent a Text that read,

"DAMN, I FELL ASLEEP.
I HOPE IT'S NOT 2 LATE."

ANOTHER LEVEL

Being a Black Woman in a World

Of little Black Boys is Rough

It's Tough

When will our Black males Grow up?

Silly me

Thinking that I had myself a Man

There he Stands

With his Toys in his Hand

I expected him to Treat me like a Woman

He Failed

Train wrecked around a Quarter til' Nine

Derailed

He Apologized

I asked him to Explain

He was Offended

I refused to let another man Use me

I'd rather suffer Rejection

Than to allow a man to Fool me

Death before letting a man

Emotionally Abuse me

I guess he chose me with Hopes of me

Being a Weak Vessel

But he learned very soon

That I wasn't on his Level

YOU CREATED ME

As I race to the Back of my Mind

Trying to find where this Relationship went Wrong

I can't help but to begin in the Beginning

Finding that there's No Ending

To this repeat Cycle of

Spending out of control

That's got me Spinning out of control

I can't even Recognize myself

What else can I do besides Cry?

I've been Crying for Days

But you have yet to offer Consolation

Because you just think that

I have something in My Eye

I'm fed up with this Veil that you have created

Veiling yourself from me

Because you think that I look Horrible

And I am Horrible

But you're the Blame

You're Horrible

We're both the Same

So don't you Dare shake your Head

Or Turn your Feet away from me

It's you who Played the Biggest part

In Creating me

I'LL NEVER LOVE AGAIN

I gave you my Heart

But you gave me your Behind to Kiss

Not Surprised...

Weighing on the thought that it was Destined

To End like this

If you never see me again

Don't miss me

You never wanted Forever anyhow

Not even when you Kissed me

I don't know why you put on your Rendition of

I'm angry that you Ran away

Truth is,

I should've Stayed away

I Befriended you

Of all of the things that I could've done

That's why it Hurts so much

Being hurt isn't Fun

But you know that... Right?

You've been Hurt before by me

But I didn't Hurt you Intentionally

It was an Accident

But you know that... Right?

Let's face it

No man could EVER Love me

Not even you

So go ahead

Be Superman for the World

And be a Villain to me

Give them More and give me Less

Rip my Heart out of my Chest

Care not about whether I Die

Because I'm Dead to you anyhow

And likewise, You're Dead to me

But always keep in Loving Memory

The Moments that I Loved you

As well as those Moments

When you Loved me

Love expired Last Night

Never to Live again

My love for you is Dead

So Rest in Peace Love

Because I'll never Love again

DAMAGED GOODS

Why do they call em' DAMAGED GOODS?
It can't be GOOD If it's DAMAGED
Been cut so many times
That it can't be Fixed with a Bandage

No cuts by Cut Buddies
There have only been Relationships
No returning to Shore
Too far under like Sunken Ships

Drunken myths is what it is when they say
There's Somebody for Everybody
Where in the Rule Book is Love
Forbidden as a Hobby

It was Mine

I fell way too many Times

Like Marijuana,

Each time it Burned a Stem from my Mind

And now

No Man wants to Deal with this

Repeated words, "I'm not Feeling this."

He finally said,

"I'm investing way too much to stay around

and just put up with this."

And he's Right

So I don't put up a Fight

To convince him that I'm Suffering

From a Past Life

Of playing the Role of a Victim

He thinks I'm No Good

I believe I'm No Good

I'm Damaged

And DAMAGED

Can't amount to

ANYTHING GOOD

NEVER LEARNED HOW TO LOVE

I'm Searching for Myself

As If I Work for the FBI

It Seems as if I Can't Find Myself

At least not with the Naked EYE

I mean...I tried...

I really did

Thought that The Plan Had Come to FRUITION

Come to find that it was an ILLUSION

Self-education the Price of Tuition

Nevertheless, I'm still on a Mission

AMBER ALERT...I'M still Missing

Trying to SPEAK unto the World

When I'M not Even Listening

Wishing to Find a trace...

Red Eyes and Puffy FACE

I Lost MYSELF along the Way

Searching for Love in a Desolate Place

ALL of this Lust has Transformed into HATE

Didn't Know that LOVE could Evaporate

So Now We're Living in a MIST

Amidst this Platform that's Emotionally Based

It Seems that My EMOTIONS

Love Me

Therefore, I have to Listen to Them

But When They Told Me to

Leave YOU Alone

I Refused to LISTEN to Them

I Ignored Them

Said Things Like…

"Oh No, I'm Just a Little Nervous"

Thought that I was Just Afraid to Fall in Love

Treaded Along a Superficial Surface

Couldn't Even Find a Purpose

Didn't We Use to Love Each Other?

Now I'd Rather PRAY for YOU

To Find Love in Another

And that's Deep…

Because I used to Pray for you to be my Husband

But When you Couldn't Walk with me…

Through the Pain…

I kind of lost Sight of all of this Trusting

Contemplated Attention Hustling…

In case you don't know what that is...

It's when your Mate is Occupied

So you Hustle attention

From other Men

That's when it hit me...

Couldn't believe what I was turning into

Had to Walk away...

Don't take it Wrong...

I did this for me and you

We're right for other people...

Wrong for One Another...

We should've been working

towards Monogamy...

Instead of Rushing to be instant Lovers

I just can't see Myself

Succumbing to ANYTHING Less

Than what I Deserve...

I understand...

It's not your Fault...

You just NEVER LEARNED HOW TO LOVE

A WOMAN'S GROWTH

I started tripping...

Started telling myself things like...

"Well, I guess I'm just Meant to be by myself...

For the Rest of my Life"

Thought that it was Cool to Succumb to being his

Woman instead of his Wife

Started believing things like...

He's going to commit...

Right now you just can't see it...

Tried to Convince myself that

such Lies were True...

In an effort to get you to believe it

I Know...

I Know...

I Know...

Looks can be Deceiving...

Nevertheless,

if I Lose this Man and end up Lonely...

I'll be Grieving

I can't say that I don't Love him

I'll never say that I never did

Can't even Front about it...

I was willing to have his Kids

Now I'm questioning if he Loves me

Wondering if he ever did

Was he just fascinated by intimacy with a good girl

Was I just a TEMPORARY Fix?

Fighting to hold back Tears…
as I Watch him with other Women
Told him, "Oh yeah, it's cool."
Acting like I'm just that Forgiving

Didn't want to become Bitter by enduring a Pain
That's Dark as Night
Therefore, I Struggle with the thought of ever…
Being a man's Wife

But I never stopped Loving him
And I probably NEVER will

I promised myself to never stop Praying for him…
Lived up to those Words…
I NEVER DID

Just because I Pray for him…

It doesn't mean that I Pray for him to Be with Me

Nevertheless, for this Mess...

I can only Blame me

I may grow Blind at times...

From Time to Time I may Stumble...

But my Mistakes are my Growth into...

Becoming a Greater Woman

FINDING LOVE

Empty…Nothing to Say…

I can't even live Right

Speechless…Can't even Think of how to Pray…

Long days and Restless nights

For me…

The Young and the Restless isn't just a Soap Opera

I'm Young…

However, I have a bus load of Problems

How did I end up Here?

Where is there for me to Go?

The man who said he Loved me

Is acting like he Doesn't even Know

It's OK to be Unsure…

Just don't Front as if you have the Answer

Opening a breeding ground for Insecurities...
So now I need an accurate Answer

And it's hard to believe that I wrote poems entitled
Blessed be the Man Who Finds a Woman Like Me
When I can't even find a Man
Who can find the Good in me

Sometimes I think to myself...
Those thoughts could be quite Rude...
I think things like...
You're supposed to be a woman?

Please...What type of woman are you?

I want to find Love...
One day I want to be Married...
Can't believe I'm STILL Single...
Nerves in my stomach feels like I Miscarried

My mind plays Tricks on me...

Saying no one will EVER Love you

A man could NEVER put you First...

No man could ever Love you

That's when I have to Dig Deep enough...

To find the Truth within myself

Truth is,

I can find love without the help of anyone else

RESIGNED LOVED

Non-existent Timing…

We are rapidly Declining

Don't Blame me for any of this…

You Forced me to consider Resigning

So while your Friends were Co-signing…

I hope they give you what you Need

Momma said if I laid down with Dogs…

I'd surely Wake up with Fleas

So now you're Peeping around Corners…

Trying to Determine my every Move…

But why?

You weren't that Concerned when I gave it all to you

See that's the thing about so called Men...

They get Comfortable with doing Nothing

Reassuring yourself of...

how many Females you can Pull

While there's a split in your Attention

How can you divide your Attention...?

And think that it's OK

Who dies over Pocket Change...

When they can live for the Bank

So go ahead...

Convince yourself that you'll find Another Me

Good Luck with that...

I'm just Relieved to have set myself Free

THE ONLY ONE PLAYING

I stopped caring what he was thinking...
Didn't mind his mind being on...
Other women this time
Figured it would mask the pain of the loss...

I was gone...
Didn't wonder whether he would try to get me back
I was thinking that maybe he thought that
this was a game...
But he was the only one playing

I was gone...
You mean to tell me that you're not intelligent to...
know when there's a downward spiral...
Or maybe you just didn't care...

Since you didn't care...

I didn't either

Therefore, find something faithful in the streets...

See if you can Trust those streets...

See if you can love those streets...

And since you stopped giving your love to me...

Go ahead and Hug and Kiss those streets

I'm Done...

Because clearly you thought that this was a game

And furthermore, in case you didn't know...

You were the only one who was Playing

A GOOD WOMAN'S BLUES

It's not Supposed to be like This...

The Warring for his Kiss...

The Battling for his Hug...

The Bickering for his Love

God Created the Lights...

Greater to Rule the Day...

Lesser to Rule the Night...

Therefore, this Battle of the Sexist...

Was supposed to be for us to Unite

As a woman...

I don't understand the Motives of a Man...

I feel like they Hate us...

I wish that thought had no room to Expand

Forgive me if I'm Wrong...
But the Answer is in High Demand
But is it against the Law...
To put a Ring on a woman's Hand

I guess I truly don't know...
What it means to be a GOOD WOMAN
They always say I'm something special...
But they always end up running

They run away from Commitment...
They run away from being Faithful...
They run away from Giving Love...
I can't understand why they're so Hateful

They seem to gravitate to women who...
Disrespect themselves in the Streets
As if a GOOD WOMAN can't be the one...
To give him what he Needs

If I lose Respect for myself...

I guess he'll give me More...

But I can't give him the Satisfaction of...

Defining me as a Whore

It's a Shame...

Because a GOOD WOMAN was all I ever wanted to be

But, I never want to be that Woman...

If she feels ANYTHING like Me

PHASE II

The Mistakes of Love

In love, sometimes we make mistakes. We sometimes say things we shouldn't, and sometimes we may even do things we shouldn't. I have learned over time that love is a testy situation. You have to learn strength and endurance to achieve such a thing. I've made my share of mistakes, but I always try to make it my business to not be a repeat offender. Sometimes, we push away blessings because we're too busy peering into the past. So I'm dedicated to looking into the future and loving the present as it unfolds.

MY MISTAKE

Another Mistake made

Yes, I do admit

Not to say that you're my Mistake

Just that I made a mistake of this

Fell too Quick

Jumped too Soon

Hopped into what I should've Saved

But what Experience would I have

If it wasn't for Choices made

Pushed you away

Slap to the Face

Watched you Hurt and Drown in Dismay

So when you were Fed up
Tired of Enough
You finally Walked away

I asked you why
But you Couldn't hear me
Correction you Wouldn't hear me

And I would Never try to Blame you for that
But I Promise to try to know how to Treat you
If God Blessed me to let you come back
They say, "Hurt people HURT people."

So I guess that's what made me Hurt you
I couldn't stop myself from Deserting
Your Love for me
Just proving that I NEVER really Deserved you

THE PEOPLE WE USED TO BE

Silent conversations

You used to be my Words

No voice across the Phone Lines

But you always allowed me to be Heard

You pushed me away Slowly

But rapidly I was Hurt

You killed my every Spirit

But you were the Epitome of my Rebirth

There will Never be a Day

That I Fall out of Love with you

Despite the many Struggles in Life

You've always pulled me through

But these days Travel by Slowly
Because there is NO you for me
Somehow, along this Journey
We forgot who we used to be

I've Walked away from you
You've Walked away from me
For so many Nights
My soul cried out to you so Desperately

You heard my Voice aloud
But you couldn't hear my Heart
Time, Distance, Pains mere Existence
Tore our Bond apart

I know that you've Cried out for me
Because you've Loved me just the same
And because I chose to Ignore your Calls
You place me as the Blame

But I was so Afraid

So terribly in Fear

That one Day I would awake

And you wouldn't be so Near

You're so Dear to me

A part of who I am

Please don't think for a Moment

That I don't Regret the Day in which I ran

I never wanted you for Money

I never wanted you for Fame

I never wanted you for your Appearance

Or for the way in which you Came

I've Loved and I've Lost

But for me it wasn't a Game

Because my Heart was Serious

The moment it called upon your Name

I'm aware that Lyrics and Verses

Will never be Enough

But I'll give you the Truth so Nakedly

So that you can possess my Love

When all else fails, I'll dry your Tears

Just so that you can see

That Happily Ever After

Lies in the people whom we used to Be

BURNED BRIDGES

I've BURNED BRIDGES in my Life

But there's one with need to be Rebuilt

Love haunts me every Night

And places a Jury before my Guilt

Stitched together like a Quilt

Are my Thoughts and Feelings for you

Set in my body like Nicotine

Are those Emotions that live for you

My Addiction...That you are

My Guide...My every Star

My glass of the most expensive Wine

That cannot be stored in Bars

I would Crawl through Tunnels

Drain my Heart through a Funnel

If it means spending life with you

And if your Heart has Grown Cold

I'll spend a Century inside of it fighting the Flu

Because I know that you'd be my Vitamin C

And Nurture me through it All

We've been here before

Just try to Remember how we've burned...

The biggest Walls

But the Bridge that Leads to you

I burned it by Mistake

Therefore, I'll piece together this Trail

Over High Waters for however long it Takes

I Pray that it's not Too Late

By the time I make it to you

If so,

My River of Tears will Cover

The Bridge rebuilt with Love for you

MY TRAIL OF TEARS

There's a Trail that leads to your Heart
And I must follow it Carefully
For if I Lose my way
There'll be NO you and me

There'll be NO you and I
Nothing but Tears for me to Cry

The Lord knows that Heaven holds NO Tears
But without you I would Die
My Heart will have NO Life

For it is you who makes it Beat
I'll walk this Trail for a thousand Miles
Sweaty palms and Blistered feet
Without a Morsel for my Soul to Eat

I'll still make it there somehow
If a stranger attempts to stop me
I'll respond with, "Not right now."

Because nothing can stop this Journey
Of capturing your Heart for Good
There is no one who could tell me
What I shouldn't or what I should
I've cried my way from the Beginning

I'll cry to the very End
Trail of Tears, don't fail me
Until my Lovers Heart I Win

THE QUIT BEFORE THE LOSS

The reason I ran from you
Can never be my Excuse
But I Pray that it offers Comfort
Please inform your Heart that it wasn't you

I Fell in Love with you
So I couldn't allow anything to go Wrong
With that being said
I left you Alone

Never thought about how you Felt...So Selfish
That I Broke my own Heart
Out of Fear that you might
Snatch away your Love

Now here I am

Pen in Hand

Desiring your Love

Wishing you were my Man

You Comforted me as I Cried

Because I somehow couldn't get used to the Fact...

That my Mother had Died

I knew that it was Draining

But you Stood there by my Side

I can't Explain the way that you Cut through...

The Yellow Tape

You didn't Judge me as so many did with

Knowledge of my Rape

You took your time

Placing my Mind into a State of Submission

Cared for me, Despite my Life

As though my Welfare was your Mission

Through Anger, Insecurities,

And even Weight Gain

You were my Umbrella

Shielding me from the Rain

Protecting me from the Pain

But ready, we never were

From me, you desired Everything

To be Alone was what I Preferred

I chose Me over You

An indefinite Cost

Because when God took my Mother,

I Loss

When the Fire took my Home,

I Loss

When God took my Sister,

I Loss

When I Lost my Virginity to Deceit,

I Loss

As I lay on that Sofa, wrapped in a Sheet

Raped, Crying, Just as a lost Sheep

I Loss

And at that point,

I couldn't Suffer you as my Loss

Because I paid my Heart to you

I owned a Part of you

My nights had No End to Darkness
My days could Not start without you
So instead of Losing you...
As I had already Loss so much

I would rather have been the Core of all of my
Undying Hurt
Your Kiss, Your Touch
The Moment that I began to Love

I fell into your Pit
I Failed your Love by way of Fear
Because it was I who Chose to Quit

CLOSED WALLS

Four of them

Standing tall like Soldiers with Guns

Closing me in Blocking my Sun

Leaving me nowhere to Run

There was No Way Out

No Doors, Sealed Ceilings, and Locked Floors

I screamed for more of you as sounds drew up

And ordered the Tears to Pour

That only caused you to Ignore me

There were No Words like Laryngitis

I spoke but I was never heard

You walked away from where my Sight is

You left me so I have No Sense

Of where anything right is

And now I've made these four walls Home

I Blocked you

Just as you had Blocked me

But to my Heart you owned the Key

I gave it to you the First Time

I allowed you to

Move into my Mind

Intertwining your Soul into Mine'

Within Due time,

I learned that I couldn't shake you

Snatched myself away

And Tried to find a way to Break you

I only made myself Miserable

By hoping for a Miracle

I had hopes of you walking Back into my Life

And allowing me to be Near to you

I thought that I was Dear to you

As I flipped through Magazines

Trying to find the Gown of a Queen

I prayed for an Alter

That would Honor you as my King

But it was only a Prayer

And as long as you're there

There will be No One to Share my all

Because only you have the Power

To enter these Closed Walls

IN LOVE WITH SOMEONE ELSE

I Love him

But I'm not IN Love with him

I'm in Love with the other

Although I shouldn't be

The one that I Love

But Refuse to be in Love

With Seems

As if he could Possibly be a Gift

But how many Gifts have you

Longed to Return?

How many Gifts have you

Retrieved the Receipt for?

Hoping that you could just get the Money

Ultimately, how many Gifts have you Given away

To your Friends because you just didn't want it?

Can't I just Break up with a Man

For not wanting him?

Is that a Good enough Reason?

Can't I just Break up with him

Because I'm in Love with Someone else?

Someone who's quite Strange

But Sincere

I Love his Gut feelings

Because when he Releases

Those Gut feelings that he has for me

I never have to Worry about them being Real

It probably wouldn't matter anyway

Because that's how much

Love I have for him

PAGES WITHIN MY NOTEBOOK

PAGES WITHIN MY NOTEBOOK

All bound together

Who ever said that my Words and Thoughts

Would All bind together?

I write my Soul between Lines

Some Simple and some Clever

Many Feelings often Change

But there are some that Last Forever

Some become Non-existent

Similar to the way you feel for me

Or the feeling of Loneliness

Embedded deep inside of me

Smells like a Smoke Filled room,

I can't Breathe

I have an Undying Love for you

But you don't Feel that way for me

And now that you're not around

I look to these Pages for Comfort

I look back to when you Cared for me

That's the Place where I Long to be

So I use my Imagination

It doesn't take much Concentration

I pretend that you still Love me

Falling for the Sensation

Love's colors are Black and White

No magical Pigmentation

But the End is only an End

Therefore, I end my Contemplation of you

Because these Pages can be quite Deceiving

Deoxygenated Words

I'm surprised I'm still Breathing

So tonight, within these Writings

I won't take a Second Look

Because No Matter how much I imagine

These will only be

PAGES WITHIN MY NOTEBOOK

WANTING A NEW HEART

Feelings Scattered across an open Floor

Am I supposed to Feel this way?

Am I supposed to Hurt because of Love?

No mistake about it

It is Love

I Love him

Would do Anything for him

Would even do More for him

Then I would do for Myself

I guess that Explains why

I Feel as Awful as I do

The feeling of being Unappreciated, I guess

And it's Sort of Not Fair to him

Because he doesn't know that I'm Feeling

Unappreciated

Would tell him

But I'm Afraid

Afraid that he would do the same as everyone else

Afraid that he would use my moment of Weakness

As a chance to Break me

And though I've been Broken enough times to see

It as Second Nature

I'm not into repeated Pain

Though I've Mended my Heart back together...

Enough times to be a Seamstress

I'm not into fixing Holes, and finding missing

Buttons, and hemming Garments...

That don't fit Quite Right

I'm not saying that

I'm looking for Perfect

But for Once,

I just want to own a NEW HEART

And not get Stuck with this Hand Me Down

That I've had since Birth

UNFORGIVEN

I wish that I could Make him Love me

The Same way that I Love him

But I've Hurt him by way of Fear

I've hurt myself by way of Tears

Never thought that I would end up Here

And at this point

All words that make way into his Ears

Are UNBELIEVABLE

My deceit wasn't on Purpose

No receipt was given at Purchase

When he Bought my Heart

So he Never returned it

It was an Original

Sometimes I wonder if he Burned it

His every thought was I

But sometimes I wonder if I Turned it

Tried to Give him the Rest of me

He wouldn't Take it

My Soul was Too Much for him

My Heart was made of Glass

His decision was to Break it

He threw it against the wall

As if it was a Basketball

And pushing him to the Rear

Was an Epic downfall

He never Forgave me for it

I can't say I Blame him

Because I know that he knows that

He can never Love me the same again

PHASE III

Never Stop Loving

After having gone through so much, I had come to the conclusion that I would never fall in love again. Then, I remembered that my entire journey wasn't something to cry over. That's when I remembered him; the man who never really gave up on me. It's almost scary how he makes it so easy for me to love again. Secretly, I never really stopped loving him.

NEVER SAY NEVER

They say, NEVER SAY NEVER

If you've NEVER before Tried

Because if you say NEVER

Then you Deliberately Lied

Once upon a time I said

I'd NEVER Fall in Love

But in this day and time

I see that I'm So in Love

I've been Hypnotized and Ostracized by Love

My Friends and Family just don't realize my Love

The Love that I see in him can be found in no other

The Love that we Possess can't be described...

By Shapes or Colors

Because this Love is Abstract

Only a few can handle that

And not enough Charisma

Can make up for what You Lack

But, he doesn't lack personality Wise

Because I see through his Soul

As I look in his Eyes

He doesn't lack in his overall Quota

From the Style of his Walk

To the width of his Shoulders

From the way that he Moves

To the Swagger of his Talk

When we're apart we're like a Black Board

With the Absence of Chalk

Blank in our ways

But together with strong Passion

An everlasting Compassion...

That never goes out of Fashion

NEVER SAY NEVER

When referring to Love

Because you would've NEVER said NEVER

If you knew how to Love

A NATURAL THING

It's too early for me to Trust you
So just Bear with me Sweetie
It's too early for me to Love you

But I'm here when you Need me
I can only Plead my Case;
It's up to you to Believe me

I want to belong to you;
Therefore, I want you to Need me

I understand that you get Irritated
When other guys Look
But they couldn't Steal me from you
If they were professional Crooks

I dare not think of us as a habitual Fling

Because my Attraction to you

Feels like A NATURAL THING

YOUR LOVE

If I could write a MILLION words

I'd write them JUST for you

Because I could only IMAGINE Living Life

Without you

I could've done what others Expected

And Played the Game by the Rules

Even if a Million guys were in the Room

You'd still be the ONE I'd Choose

Everyone has Flaws

And NO ONE is Deemed PERFECT

I speak SUCCESS into our Future

So all of these Struggles will be WORTH IT

I know that you've been Hurt
And even taken for Granted
But there's NO WOMAN who Loves you MORE...
Walking the Face of this PLANET

We never seem to Argue
But sometimes we Disagree
But we both have reached the Agreement that...
God has UNITED you and me

Sometimes things get in our way
And Discourage us quite a bit
Of course I get the Urge to rest
But never will I Quit

We'll always need the Lord
If we DESIRE to stay together
LUST is Temporary
But LOVE last Forever

There may be many Stumbling Blocks

And Things to get in our way

But when things get too hard for us

We'll get on our knees and PRAY

"I LOVE YOU"

Are the most Precious Words

That anyone could Say

And YOUR LOVE is the most Precious Gift

That you give to me Every Day

MY HEART

A Heart is a Blood Pump
One of the most vital Organs in the Human body
And for you to take something so Dear
Away from me is quite Ungodly

You're the Thief of my Night
The Villain of my Fight
The Smudge on my Wall
After I painted it White

You took MY HEART
After knowing how much it meant to me
How could you leave me Lifeless
And Plugged to these Machines?

A Tube is down my Throat

I can't Breathe on my own

I need you to Live

You are my Lungs

All of the Power on this Earth has stood still

I need you to keep me Strong

I'm on the verge of Dying which means

I'm on the verge of Living

You are my Soul Mate

And I will spend my life Giving

My life to Loving you

And the Heavens will document this as

Concrete Proof

But I still haven't Forgiven you
And I probably Never Will
Because the way you stole my Heart
Is the same way that I was Killed

I no longer want to Live
Because I'm content with my Soul

And I'm content with you as a Mate
If you ever decide to hand MY HEART back
You would then be Too Late

Will God place a New Heart into a Dead body?
You'll never be God
But to me your Love is godly

Because I know that you Love me

Like Christ loves His church

I may be Second in your Life

But only God comes First

So when your Arrow was in my Chest

My clothes became Soggy

Because I bleed for Hours upon Hours

And it was you who Shot me

The Heart that has Lost me

Is the same Heart that found you

That Heart is NO LONGER mine

Because MY HEART belongs to you

In a binding Covenant between God and I

MY HEART belongs to you

Until the Day that I DIE

SOME DAY

I was Wrong,

I admit it, I was Wrong

Something in the back of my mind

had convinced me That I was Strong

Strong enough to Live this Life without you

Strong enough to Breathe without you

Strong enough to Tell the World

That this Poem isn't about you

You taught me how to Open up

At times when I was Choking up

You taught me how to take this Cover off

And Expose my Love

You taught me what it meant to

Accept the Inner Being

You taught me how to Miss you

Before I ever thought about Leaving

But I did it Anyway

Expecting to find a Way

To hide from the Feeling that would

Haunt me on Today

Secretly I Pray

To love you again SOMEDAY

I just hope that SOMEDAY

Isn't equivalent to Too Late

LOVE IS

Barely Breathing

Constantly Sleeping

Ill from something Strange

That seems to live Deep In

Nose Burning

Head Turning

I'm on the Axis of something

That will never be Funny

Weird weather, one-day Cold

And the next day Sunny

Cough syrup

Lemon with a hint of Honey

A cold in the Summer

Is like a heat stroke in the Winter

And Love is that thought

That you forgot to Remember

Love is that Illness that Sneaks up on you

Love is that Bug that Creeps up on you

Love is so Cold that Vitamin C can't cure it

Love is so harsh that no one can Endure

The Fight that it puts up

The Beat that it puts down

The Energy drawn in

The Ambience it puts out

Again love is so Cold that...

Vitamin C can't cure it

Love is so Bold that outsiders would...

Pay to tour it

UNCONDITIONAL

He loves me in the Morning

When I'm not all that Pretty

He loves me in the Moments

When I'm not all that Witty

He loves me when my Laugh

Gets a bit too Silly

A million Roses are in the Garden

But he still loves his Lily

He loves me before

I make appointments at the Salon

He loves me in the Mirror

Before my make-up is Done

He loves me when he only hears me Breathe

On the Phone

There were a million in the Crowd

But he saw me Alone

He loves me when I'm Down

And cannot find a way up

He loves me when I'm not feeling Skinny enough

He loves me Tenderly although I know it is Tough

I'm Blessed to have his Love

Although you see it as Luck

He loves me for the fact that

I'm One of a Kind

He says that I exceed Millions

And worth far more than a Dime

He loves me like a thought

Because I stay on his Mind

His love is UNCONDITIONAL

And doesn't Waiver through Time

A SECOND CHANCE

Always found a Place for you
Although I said I was Over you

Lies to Myself
Grew bad for my Health
I poured you out of my Cup until nothing was Left
To my Soul it brought Death

And now, here again
You Stand
A SECOND CHANCE

I had to Grow into a Woman
To accept you as a Man
I hope you Understand

You used to come to my Rescue

But you eventually got Tired

I feel you

I had you wondering when the

Bull was to Expire

I would do it all for you

Even build an Empire

And at this very Moment

I don't have to force the Drama to Retire

I know that you're unsure about

Whether I'm here to sit Still

If for no one Else

For you, I will

Promises are often Broken

But I'll prove myself True

And I don't have to State your Name

To let you know this is about you

THE SONG OF OUR LOVE

How was I to know that you were

The Best part of me?

How Silly of me to think that

Feelings Diminish over time

Running away as if there was

Somewhere to Run to

Ironically

I always Managed to

Bump right back into you

A Heart with NO Beat cannot Survive

But you provided my Beat as if you were

A Drummer in a Marching Band

Constructing your Notes in a manner that

Only made Sense to you at the Moment

And as time Passed,

You began to Perfect your Craft

Only then did it all began making

Sense to me

So I grabbed my Saxophone and began Playing

As though there was no Tomorrow

Because we Both knew that

If we Didn't play together

There Wasn't going to be a Tomorrow

And now here we are Playing

The Music of our Souls

Allowing the world to Listen and to Dance

And to slowly Drift into a Land

Where Music matters the Most

There are no Lyrics

Because Words no longer Express

And this isn't a mere Performance

It's a Life within Itself

The only way that it Dies is

If one of us stops Playing

So don't let your hands Grow

Weary in Beating

And I won't let my Lungs

Run out of Breath

For if either of us shall Fail

This song shall NEVER

Be Played Again

OVERTHROWN QUEEN

Heart taken

Mind as well

Can't rule my Castle anymore

Challenged Beyond my ability

And Yes

It was I who Opened the Door

Allowed him to be the King of my World

I can't Leave Because I'm Powerless

Too Emotional I Love Him

And my Love for him cannot be Surpassed

Enslaved is what I am

I no Longer want to be Free

AN OVERTHROWN QUEEN

The reigning King possesses this
Type of Hold on me

Although I haven't Lost my Title
My Heart I no longer Own
A Queen without a Heart
IS A QUEEN DESTINED TO BE OVERTHROWN

But the King is quite the Ruler
He deserves to be on the Thrown

But if he ever Leaves
THE QUEEN WILL BE OVERTHROWN

SOMETHING ABOUT YOUR LOVE IS BEAUTIFUL

Your eyes are the Piercing shade of Beauty

There is something more than Pigmentation

That catches my Attention

As I peer into the Windows of your Soul

I see a sky filled with a Glow of Magnificence

I see a River of Brilliance

That only Flows when the Heart demands it to

I see a field of Lovely which Blooms

In the Weather of Love

Yes, I see Love

Your Lips are the Smoothest touch of Beauty

There lies something more than a Kiss

I see an Expression of Wonder

Yes, your Lips are Wonderful

With your Lips,

You are able to Communicate Thoughts

That have been Buried beneath your Mind

Secrets long to be Exposed over time

As your Lips meet Mine's

The Puzzle Pieces resemble

A perfect fit Exactly at the Lines

On your Lips,

Expressive Beauty is Shown

Yes, I see your Expressions

Your Nose is the strongest Shade of Beauty
I allow the Tip of my Nose to
Gently Touch the Tip of yours

Activating pores of Glory
As your Glorious skin Pretends to be Strong, Stern,
and Sturdy

You become Tickled and that Smile of yours
Stretch for Miles across your Face
Informing me that I'm in a Place of Safety
I can be Comfortable because
I know that you're Pleased with my Company

Your ears are a Beautiful Portal
Allowing voices to Enter
A Safe Haven that causes you to Remember

There lie the Memories of Us

An anchor for Trust

Your Boat of sound only Tolerates

Beautiful Noises

And every one of your Choices is Beautiful

Because you choose to Hear

More than Sweet Nothings

And that is what makes your

Love Beautiful

GLASS OF WINE

Half full or Half empty

Depends upon the Eye

I hope this Wine originated

From your Vines help to Fight this feel of Shy

As I look into your Eyes

I see more than Just the Iris

A Sip of your Love is Priceless

I glance at my Watch but this Moment is Timeless

Time fades but I long to Rewind this

I place my Lips where your Wine is

You give me Kisses of great Expense

I drift into the great Immense

Your Glass is big enough for me

Greedy is what I will not be

Only if this Wine contains your Name

Will everything be Good with me

Traces of Cherry Red Wine lies upon your Skin

Let's not Pretend

We both Recognize your Wine by its Scent

In a State of Intoxication

There's no Mascoto or Merlot that

Can offer this Sensation

It's fine;

I'll allow your Wine to Overpower my Mind

Because from your Vine Flows Love

Into this Glass as my Wine

ACCEPTING HIM

So enticing is his Love

I love the way he Loves me

But you don't seem to Approve of him

Asking what is it that I might Lose for him

To help you see the bigger Picture

I'm head to head against the Rules for him

He wants me in his Life

And that is all I EVER Wanted...

He's no Phony

So why should I View him as my Opponent

If he's not as Christian as you think that he should be

Trust me...I got this

Allow me to Pray for him Fervently

Because only God can make him Spotless

I won't allow you to Force your homemade Laws

Upon my Life

What is it to you if I choose to be his Wife?

Do you suddenly have the Power

to save me on Judgment day?

For you, Hell may be only a day away

So stay fancy

Continue to be proud about yourself

Are you concerned about me...

Or only that feeling that you give yourself?

What else will it take for you to Love the way I Love

I guess the simple act of Acceptance for you

Will NEVER be Enough

LOVE MADE A LIAR OUT OF ME

If Love came in a Jar

I would Store it for the Winter

Because the Heart is at

Its Coldest in the days of Mid-December

I love you Hopelessly, Desperately, and Pathetically

I'm completed by what you Provide

You're the sound to my Symphony

An Opera beautifully Song

Are your Words to my Soul

So I give a standing Ovation until

My Applause stir up your Soul

You truly mean the World to me

Although you Require so much of me

I can't Quit or Give up on you

Because you've always saw the Best in me

Remember when I said that All Hope was Gone

I thought that we would Never be

But Love and All of its Ways

Made a Liar out of me

AGAIN

I hadn't Felt it in a while

At that point,

I thought that it had gone Out of Style

Undoubtedly,

I thought that it had Forgotten about me

I Played the part of the Woman

Seated on the Front Porch

I Spoke viciously about it as it Stepped

Outside of its Door

I Hated it because I thought that it Hated me

I Screamed to the Top of my Lungs

"What have you ever done for me?"

On our initial Meeting, it made me feel Jittery

It never returned my Calls

It literally made a Fool of me

That wasn't very Cool to me

Tears Streamed down my Face

Thoughts raced through my Mind

It gently told my Conscience

How sorry it was

I believed its Lies

It told me that it was OK for him

To Knock the hell out of me

Hell was Living inside of me

It Provoked him to Lie to me

I had it all Wrong

It Convinced me that it was Wrong

For me to ask him Questions like, "Where are you?"

"Who are you with?"

I'm beyond Recognition

My Clothes won't even Fit

I can't even Enjoy how Great it is

Worried about the Devastation of Learning

That it's Faker than a Counterfeit bill

While spending it at the Register

It registered to me that I was Cuffed

Was it not Enough for me to have taken the Risk?

Believing that it was all Supposed to be like this

I felt it after the Tears

I felt it after the Pain

I believed Betty Wright when she Sang

No Pain, No Gain

Let it Rain, let it Rain

After Five heart beats

I was Destined to be Changed

As my nerves Dropped

Into the bottom of my Stomach

I realized that the "IT" which I was Referring to

Wasn't really it

And what Happened back then Wasn't really this

So I bowed my Head and said a Prayer

Tossed my Head back

And looked directly into the Air

Thinking that I could Give what

Possibly could be the authentic "IT"

a real chance

I dreamed of Romance

While removing these pants of Lies

Along with this Shirt

That causes my Desire for "IT" to Die

I was Stripped down to the naked Truth

"IT" was Beautiful

And there "IT" was

I was again in Love

FOREVER

He said, "You think too Much"

I said, "I don't think Enough"

If over thinking makes you Weak

Does under thinking make you Tough?

I Analyzed every area and every Aspect of him

Thinking about his Demeanor

Made me gain Respect for him

Because it Certainly wasn't the lighter Skin

Nice Ride and Nice Ends

Fresh Sneakers in the Summer

In the Winter Fresh Tims

It's not even for the fact that he Gazes into my Eyes

And Smiles with a Ray of Cheer

Or for the fact that

He constantly Whispers Sweet Nothings in my Ear

I was attracted by the fact that

He made me Feel like fine China

Wanting me by my Intelligence

And NOT by my Vagina

He gets me Right when I'm Wrong

He doesn't Lure me by way of the Tongue

Sometimes he Clenches his Teeth together

Sometimes he quotes Songs

"I picture you and me starting a Family"

This is no Fantasy

He really did quote Jagged Edge to me

I really must Admit he had gotten into my Head
He looked upon my Face
My Cheeks were Rosy Red

He said, "Baby girl those are only thoughts
I'm not rushing you to Spread your Legs
Now, don't get me wrong Boo
I really do want you

And if it's Wrong
I'll take the Chair, Walk the Plank,
And even Stand before an Army for you

But Baby, I'm trying to Chill
This is what it is
I want you to make me Wait
Before you even Give me your Kiss

Because I know that it is Precious
Deeply valued at every Measure
I've been Searching for what you Got
Like a deeply buried Treasure

So when I get it,
I'm going to Treasure it,
Preserve it, and Cherish it

Please know that I want this thing for Life
I'll get down on my Knees and Marry it

I really Love you
Would never Disrespect you
Even if I was Taken away from this Earth
I still wouldn't Neglect you

I would come back in Spirit
Just to let you know that you're Safe
And I would Die a Second Death
If I was Pried away from your Grace

I'm not Rushing anything
For we should Grow together
Why Rush it anyway
When we both have Forever"

MY BLESSING

Angels glow

But you Radiate

You're more than my Angel

You're my Fate

You're my Excuse when I'm Late

You make me reciprocate Hate over Love

Placing Love over Hate

Eliminating all Feelings

That are Irrelevant to what I Feel for you

What is this that I Feel for you?

I looked down and my Hands

Were covered in a red Substance...

So I washed my Hands in a sense of Urgency

It looked like Paint

But it wasn't

Found out that it was bloody Love

The life that Breathes in Loving

I only Touched where there was Skin

You Knocked, I let you in

I didn't write the Play

So I didn't play the Role

I wasn't very Fond of a Pretend

So I made Amends and Finally said Amen

Because God knows that you're my Blessing

But if you ever become my Sin

You'd still be my Confession

A NEVER-ENDING LOVE

He Oxygenated my Words

That's why I Wrote about him

He was my Warmth in the Cold

I just couldn't do without him

I know this sound like Nothings

Sweeter than Hershey's kisses

But this Required more than an Ear

I needed his Heart to Listen

Made plenty sense

The way he Wrapped his Love around me

Passionate intermissions

He broke away just to allow me

To kiss him Softly

Yet Embrace him Roughly

Similar to a Heavenly Sin

Or a beautiful Ugly

Make no Mistake about it

I was into him so Deeply

He never left me Lonely

I needed him to Keep me

I wanted him to Say how much he Needed me

Enough for him to Train his Lungs

To Breathe me

Phlebotomy...

I drew his Blood to see if he would Bleed me

If the Earth ceases Rotation

To where we're Forced to pause in Time
It would Confirm the fact that Everything
Has an Ending except for our Love
And the Equator's line

Our Love is drawn Around
Our Love draws Wonders down
Our Love keeps everything that God
Has tied together Bound

I want to need his Love Forever
On any and every Level
If this Love means Victory
Then he Truly is my Medal

I'm high off of his Heart
Don't want to Land on Sober
Don't know where we Began

But I Cringe at the thought of Over
I long for him Over and Over again
And an Ending
Will never ever be a part of the Plan

YOUR PRESENCE

I woke up with you on my Mind
Hard to get the Gist of things with you
Occupying my Time

But you know I don't Mind
Because you're so Special to me
I don't know where I'd be if you ever Left me Lonely

You give my Life a world of Meaning
You're the Book that I get lost in Reading

You and I...Here tonight
What a Passion filled Meeting
Can't imagine seeing tomorrow's Sunrise
With peachy Skies

Without your Magnificent presence
You're the most Wonderful man alive

TOPIC OF DISCUSSION

Topic of Discussion (hand raises)

Please save your Questions

'Til after this Discussion

("But") Hun please

The Topic is not in Question

I'm extremely Frustrated

By your Excuses

Which are Words that amount to Nothing more than

How you're trying to Convince me of how your Love

For me is Real

("But") Kill

That Line of How you think I'm the Best deal

That's ever been Presented to you

Do you tell the Truth to your Boos in the Street?
Because you're sure as Hell not Presenting
Those truthful Truths to me

("Well") Well what?
What in the hell you saying Well for?
I just can't Understand why

I put up with any of your hell for?
What type of Woman have I become?
What have I Fell for?

I've failed again
So do I need to tell More?

("I love you")
All you do is make Excuses
Hold up
Wait

What did you just Say?

("I said I Love you")

And even though you're talking Trash

I Love you Anyway

You're the Last one that I think of

At the End of the Day

And the One I want to

Wake up looking Square in the Face")

But

("No need to Explain this or try to Explain that

I get it

You're making me Pay for another man's Bag

But it's Cool

Because Baby I'll get on a Payment Plan

Until I can Pay Off the Price

Of putting that Band on your Hand

I'm a Man

I understand the Topic of Discussion

And you don't have to ask if I Love you

For me to Answer the Question")

Closed Discussion

UNDEFILED SHEETS

It's late

And there's that feeling again

That crazy feeling in my chest

That makes me want to feel a man

So it dawns on me

That this was my choice

To be alone

No voice in my home

But I never wanted to be lonely

I was only trying to do what was best for me

Because we only created a pile of stress for me

Never thought that I would be here again

Watching the blades on my ceiling fan

And wondering if they ever knew...

How much they favored my life

Dressed up in all of their pretty with nowhere to go
Standing in one place but spinning out of control
Sort of reminding me of Marilyn Monroe
But afraid to be that daring
Afraid you'd see me as a whore

So many rules and regulations
To the rim with complications
Afraid that if you touch me I'd start creating
lubrication

I can't believe I just said that to you
And it's okay for you to desire what I want to do

But we're living in double standard land
I'm a woman
You're a man
And society will slaughter me if they see that they
can

So tonight

There'll be NO CALLS, NO TEXT,

Equivalent to NO SEX

I'm a woman

And my strongest asset is deprivation

I've never been anorexic

But I've never seen it in men

And I'd rather starve this urge

Than to look desperate for giving in

Because before I go there

I want my partner to care enough for me

To be before my eyes when I awake from my sleep

I know that I'm only human

And I know that makes me weak

But I would rather be alone

Before I DEFILE MY NEW SHEETS

WISH UPON A STAR

I wonder if the stars really hold wishes

Because if they do,

I have a wish that needs to be granted

I wonder if a crystal ball could fall...

from the walls of the sun

Or better yet, could a genie travel from another planet

I planned it

You know...Life

The plan was for things to go right

Sunny days with cool breezes and timid title waves

But it seems that my Dreams hold Stormy Nights

I know that the songs we Learned in Grade School

Seemed cool

A fixation of the Mind

Felt like the use of new tools

But someone should have told me that
Twinkle Twinkle Little Star was a song designed
For children and fools

I held on to the thought of the stars twinkling off
Country settings of new beginnings
As new moons formed in fall
I thought I had it all

But where is that one kiss
Sweeter than peppermints lying in a candy dish
So, I clenched my hands tightly together
Until it made the perfect fit
I prayed to God that the stars held a wish

About the Author

Ardreana Thompson is the author of The Pen God Gave Me: The Diary of my Soul and this is her second title. She was born on February 6, 1989 and was raised in the small town of Camden, AL.

She is an established Spoken Word Artist and has worked as a background artist on the set of the movie "Selma". While spending time in Atlanta, GA, she was presented the opportunity to open for Natalie "Floacist" Stewart of the nationally known group Floetry. She has also opened for local stage plays as well as spoken at Outreach events targeting young women affected by issues within the community.

Ardreana graduated from Wilcox Central High School, Camden, AL in 2007.

She has worked as a Marketing Director for Jazzy Kitty Publishing and as a songwriter for Comradery Records in Orlando, FL.

She is a member of National Council for Negro Women.

www.ingramcontent.com/pod-product-compliance
Lightning Source LLC
Chambersburg PA
CBHW070613300426
44113CB00010B/1517